W9-BDE-107

COUNTRY TOPICS
FOR CRAFT PROJECTS

GREAT BRITAIN

RICHARD AND SHEILA TAMES

Illustrated by Teri Gower

FRANKLIN WATTS

NEW YORK • CHICAGO • LONDON • TORONTO • SYDNEY

This symbol appears on some pages throughout this book. It indicates that adult supervision is advisable for that activity.

Library of Congress Cataloguing-in-Publication Data

Tames, Richard.
Great Britain / Richard and Sheila Tames.
p. cm. -- (Country topics for craft projects)
Includes index.
ISBN 0-531-14313-9
1. Handicraft--Great Britain--Juvenile literature. 2. Great Britain--Social life and customs--Juvenile literature. [1. Great Britain--Social life and customs.] I. Tames, Sheila. II. Title. III. Series.
TT57.T36   1994
745.5--dc20   93-49724
                                              CIP
                                              AC

© Franklin Watts 1994

Franklin Watts
95 Madison Avenue
New York, NY 10016

10 9 8 7 6 5 4 3 2 1

Paperback edition published in 1995
ISBN 0-531-15275-8

Editor: Hazel Poole
Designer: Sally Boothroyd
Photography: Peter Millard
Artwork: Teri Gower
Picture research: Juliet Duff

Printed in the United Kingdom

All rights reserved

Contents

Introducing Great Britain

How do you do? In Great Britain, that's the polite way of saying "hello." Before you start to explore, here are a few useful facts about the country.

FLYING THE FLAG

The Union flag (also known as the Union Jack) was invented for use on ships in 1603 when England and Scotland began to be ruled by the same monarch. It originally combined the flags of England (a red cross on white) and Scotland (a diagonal white cross on dark blue). In 1801 a diagonal red cross on white was added for Ireland which was ruled by Britain at that time. Wales has its own separate flag of white and green bands with a red dragon.

GREAT BRITAIN IN THE WORLD

Great Britain is made up of three countries, England, Wales, and Scotland. Great Britain and Northern Ireland make up the United Kingdom, along with various island groups such as the Scilly Isles, Hebrides, Shetland Islands, and Orkney Islands. Great Britain covers an area of 88,795 sq mi (229,979 sq km) (England 50,363 sq mi/130,439 sq km; Scotland 30,414 sq mi/78,772 sq km; and Wales 8,018 sq mi/20, 768 sq km). It lies in western Europe, surrounded by the Atlantic Ocean, Irish Sea, North Sea, and the English Channel. London is the capital of Great Britain, with Edinburgh and Cardiff the capital cities of Scotland and Wales respectively.

A CONSTITUTIONAL MONARCHY

Britain is a constitutional monarchy. The head of state is Queen Elizabeth II. She is also head of the Commonwealth that unites fifty countries which used to be governed by Britain.

Parliament is made up of two houses – the House of Commons and the House of Lords. The prime minister is the leader of the government.

GOD SAVE THE QUEEN

Britain was the first country in the world to have a national anthem. In its present form it dates from 1745. There is a separate Welsh national anthem – *He Wlad Fy Nhadau* (Land of My Fathers) – which dates from 1856. Although not a national anthem as such, Scots often sing *Scotland the Brave* at sports events.

MONEY AND STAMPS

The basic unit of currency is the pound, written £. The pound is divided into 100 pence (p). You can get banknotes for the following amounts – 50, 20, 10, and 5 pounds – and there are coins for £1, 50, 20, 10, 5, 2, and 1p. Scotland has different banknotes from the rest of Britain, including a note for £1.

On the edge of the coins, the letters D.G.REG.F.D. always appear after the queen's name. These stand for the Latin words *Dei Gratia Regina Fidei Defensor*, which means "By the Grace of God, Queen, Defender of the Faith."

Modern postage stamps were invented in Britain in 1840. The first was called the "Penny Black." Because Britain was the first country to have stamps, it is the only country in the world that does not have its name on them.

KEEP TO THE LEFT

In Britain you drive on the left-hand side of the road, so the steering wheel is on the right. Britain was the first country in the world to have a "rule of the road." It was introduced to avoid confusion on London Bridge. Keeping to the left meant that if a traveler was attacked by an oncoming rider, he wouldn't have to lean sideways across his horse to fight back with his sword or pistol.

Say it yourself!

English	Welsh	Gaelic
Welcome!	Croeso!	Fáilte!
Language	Laith	Caint
Car	Car	Gluaisteán
Money	Arian	Airgead

Around Britain

There are many different parts of Britain to visit – the rich, green countryside, the hilly Lake District and Peak District, the flat Fens of East Anglia, the windswept uplands of Dartmoor, and the mountainous Highlands of Scotland and Snowdonia in Wales.

Average temperatures		
Place	January	July
Edinburgh	38°F (3°C)	59°C (15°C)
Plymouth	41°F (5°C)	61°F (16°C)
Cardiff	40°F (4°C)	61°F (16°C)

BRITISH GEOGRAPHY

Britain's landscape is pleasant rather than spectacular. The country is generally flat and dry in the south and east, hilly and wetter towards the north and west. The highest peak in Scotland is Ben Nevis 4,406 ft (1,343 m), in Wales, Snowdon 3,560 ft (1,085 m), and in England, Scafell Pike 3,210 ft (978 m). The longest rivers are the Severn 180 mi (290 km), Thames 210 mi (338 km), and Trent 170 mi (274 km).

No part of Britain is more than 68 mi (110 km) from the sea. Thanks to warm ocean currents, Britain's climate is milder than that of its neighbors on the same latitude. However, the weather is also very changeable.

CANARY WHARF

London's old Docklands area has now become Europe's biggest building site as its old warehouses are converted into offices and gleaming new buildings are put up beside them. At the heart of all this is the Canary Wharf Tower – at 800 ft (244 m) and 50 stories high, it is Britain's tallest building.

THE COTSWOLDS

This upland region lies between Oxford and Bath. It is picture-postcard England at its best and a favorite day trip for tourists from London. In the Middle Ages, the area grew rich on sheep farming and making woolen cloth. Villages like Burford and market towns like Bradford-on-Avon and Chipping Camden are famous for their thatched cottages, huge Gothic "wool churches," and elegant houses made of honey-colored limestone.

THE LAKE DISTRICT

Around 1800 the dramatic landscape of this part of northwest England inspired the "Lake Poets" – Wordsworth, Coleridge, and Southey. Today the area is protected as a national park and relies heavily on tourism. The peaks around the market-town of Keswick attract climbers and hikers while lakes, such as Windermere and Ullswater, are popular for sailing and waterskiing. The home of the children's writer Beatrix Potter also attracts many visitors.

THE GREAT GLEN

This impressive valley is more than 60 miles (97 km) long and divides Scotland diagonally between northwest and southeast. Ben Nevis looms over the southern end, while historic Inverness stands at the north. Between 1803 and 1847, the Caledonian Canal was cut to link the four lochs (lakes) which lie along the Glen. This made it possible for boats to sail from the Irish Sea to the North Sea.

THE MIDLANDS

The "heart of England" is dominated by a belt of industrial cities running from Birmingham, Coventry, and Wolverhampton in the west to Leicester and Nottingham in the east. But it also contains such historic treasures as Warwick Castle and Stratford-upon-Avon, the birthplace of William Shakespeare.

EAST ANGLIA AND THE FEN COUNTRY

East Anglia is made up of the three counties of Norfolk, Suffolk, and Essex. The Fen country consists of marshes, drained by dikes and canals, stretching from Cambridge to Lincolnshire. Together these areas account for some of Britain's richest agricultural land. The main crops are wheat, barley, sugar beet and vegetables. The flat, silent landscape and huge cloud-filled skies were the main inspiration for England's greatest painter – John Constable.

WALES

The valleys of South Wales used to be famous for their coal mines and steelworks. Now there are many modern electronics factories. North Wales has far fewer people, but farming and tourism are important there.

Language and Dialect

BRITISH ENGLISH?

There is no such thing as a "British accent." Every part of the country has its own way of speaking English. "BBC English" is based on the speech of educated people from the south of England. Most British people can guess where someone comes from by the way he or she speaks. Apart from accents, there are many words which are only used in a particular part of the country and are hardly heard outside it. A Yorkshire native might use the word "gradely" to describe something excellent, while a Scot would call it "braw," and a Geordie (someone from Newcastle) would say "canny."

THE NORTH

There is no single northern accent. People from Liverpool, Leeds, and Newcastle all speak quite differently from one another. But there are some general differences between northern and southern English. For example, people in the south pronounce "bath" and "path" as if they were spelled "barth" and "parth." Northerners pronounce the "a" the same as in the word "cat."

Northern road signs

Southern road signs

Say it in Scots!
tae – to
wee – little
gey – very
ken – know
wadne – would not
kirk – church
bairn – child
aye – yes
burn – stream

CELTIC LANGUAGES

Welsh, Gaelic and Cornish all belong to the Celtic family of languages. Cornish died out around 1800, although teachers still run classes for local people interested in learning it. Gaelic is spoken by about 80,000 people in the west of Scotland and especially on its off-shore islands. Welsh has equal status with English in Wales, which means that road signs and official documents are in both languages. Many schools teach all their lessons in Welsh and there is a Welsh Television channel. About 500,000 people speak Welsh.

Understanding Welsh Place Names

aber – river mouth
bryn – hill
dol – meadow
llan – church
porth – harbor
rhyd – stream/ford

ASIAN LANGUAGES

Cities such as Bradford and Leicester have large numbers of inhabitants whose families originally came from India and Pakistan and still speak Hindi, Urdu, Punjabi, and Gujarati. The people in Chinese communities of London and Liverpool come from around Hong Kong and speak Cantonese. In Tower Hamlets, the London docks area, the most important languages after English are Bengali and Somali.

Food and Drink

Kent is known as the "garden of England" and is famous for apples, cherries, and hops. Most of Britain's fish comes through the east coast ports of Yarmouth, Hull, and Grimsby. Scotland is the home of salmon and whisky, and lamb is the national dish of Wales. Laverbread (cooked seaweed) is also eaten in Wales. Cider apples come from the orchards in the south west, from Devon to Herefordshire. Watercress is a local speciality in Hampshire. There are more than thirty different local kinds of cheese, such as Caerphilly, Wensleydale, Stilton, and Red Leicester.

Outside bars and in many vacation areas, there are often stands selling seafood such as jellied eels and whelks or cockles. These are eaten with pepper and vinegar.

PUB GRUB

Many people eat at pubs (public houses) at lunchtime and in the evenings. The menu selections usually include:

Ploughman's lunch – bread, cheese, pickles and salad
Shepherd's pie (also known as Cottage pie)– minced meat and vegetables topped with mashed potato and grated cheese.
Bangers & mash – sausages and mashed potato, often served with fried onions or baked beans
Cornish pasty – a semi circular pastry stuffed with minced meat, potato, and onion
Steak & kidney pie – stewed steak and kidneys topped with crisp puff pastry (In some tourist areas, this is often steak and mushroom pie because some people will not eat kidneys.) Many of these dishes are eaten with English mustard – which is very hot!

10

For many families, the main meal of the week is Sunday lunch, perhaps roast beef with Yorkshire pudding. Takeout meals are also very popular, and most towns have a selection of Indian, Italian, Chinese, and Greek restaurants to choose from.

Fish and chips is the classic British takeout food. It became popular in the 1860s when railroads began to bring fresh fish straight from the east coast to the great inland cities overnight. Traditionally, the fish and chips were covered with salt and malt vinegar and, using your fingers, eaten right out of the newspaper they were wrapped in.

THE GREAT BRITISH BREAKFAST

Most people have only cereal or toast for breakfast during the week, but some still have a full-cooked breakfast. A standard "full English breakfast" might consist of:

> *Cereal/Grapefruit*
>
> *Bacon and eggs (fried or scrambled)*
> *with mushrooms, beans, grilled tomatoes,*
> *fried bread, sausages*
>
> *Toast and marmalade*
>
> *Tea/Coffee/Fruit juice*

In Scotland, porridge is the traditional first course – eaten with salt, not sugar.

BEER AND WHISKY

British-style beer, made with hops, is known as "bitter." There is also a black beer with a thick, creamy head, known as "stout." This originally came from Ireland.

Whisky is the national drink of Scotland and is Britain's most valuable single export product.

Say it yourself!

English	Welsh	Gaelic
food	bwyd	biadh
breakfast	brecwast	biadh maidne
porridge	uwd	lite
water	dŵr	uisge
egg	wy	ugh
kitchen	cegin	tigh-cócaireachd
lamb	oen	uan

A Taste of Britain

Here are some traditional recipes for you to try . . .

WELSH RABBIT

1 Put the cheese and milk into a thick-bottomed pan. Heat the mixture gently and keep stirring until it melts into a thick cream.

2 Add the butter, pepper, salt, and mustard.

3 Raise the temperature a bit and keep stirring. The mixture should be hot, but do not let it boil.

4 Put the toast into an ovenproof dish and pour the cheese mixture over it.

5 Carefully place the dish under the broiler until it starts to brown.

6 Remove and serve at once.

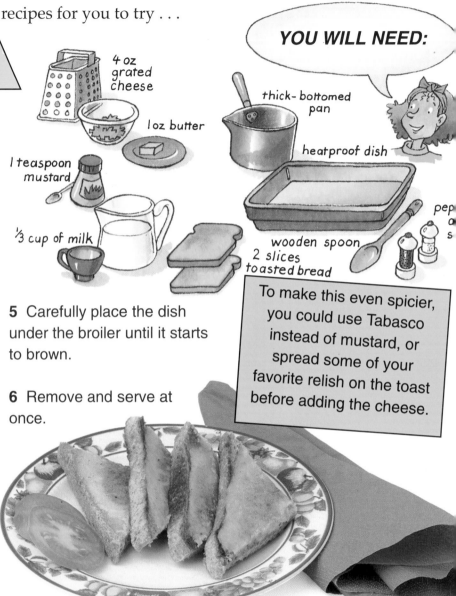

YOU WILL NEED:

4 oz grated cheese

1 oz butter

1 teaspoon mustard

⅓ cup of milk

thick-bottomed pan

heatproof dish

wooden spoon

2 slices toasted bread

pepper and salt

To make this even spicier, you could use Tabasco instead of mustard, or spread some of your favorite relish on the toast before adding the cheese.

TIME FOR TEA!

The traditional 4 o'clock tea used to consist of sandwiches, scones, fruitcake, sponge cake, and dainty pastries.

MAKING TEA

Heat the water (don't fill the kettle too full!) and pour a small amount into a teapot to warm it. Swirl the water around and then pour it out. Using fresh loose tea, place one teaspoonful of tea for each person into the pot, and then add "one for the pot." When the water is boiling, pour it into the warmed teapot. Stir once and let sit for two minutes. Pour the tea into a cup with cold milk to taste.

SCONES

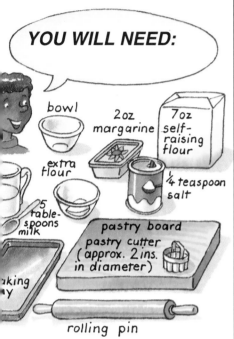

YOU WILL NEED:

bowl
2oz margarine
7oz self-raising flour
extra flour
¼ teaspoon salt
5 table-spoons milk
pastry board
pastry cutter (approx. 2 ins. in diameter)
baking tray
rolling pin

1 Sift the flour and salt into a bowl and cut in the margarine.

2 Gradually add the milk to make a soft dough (not too sticky!).

3 Turn out the mixture onto a board dusted with flour and roll it out until it is $1/3$ inch (1 cm) thick.

4 Using the cutter, cut out circles until all the dough has been used up.

SANDWICH IDEAS

Tea time sandwiches should be dainty and made with thinly sliced bread. Some people cut the crusts off or cut the sandwiches into strips about 2 inches (5 cm) wide. Here are some ideas for fillings:

Cucumber Slice the cucumber very thinly. Soak the slices in a little white vinegar and drain, then place them between two slices of bread.

Egg Hard-boil an egg and let it cool completely. Mash it with a little mayonnaise and pepper. You can also add finely chopped parsley or onion.

Sardine Remove any large bones. Mash and spread the fish, and add thinly sliced cucumber.

5 Place the circles on a cookie sheet that has been lightly greased with margarine.

6 Bake in the oven at 400°F/200°C/Gas mark 6 for about 12 to 14 minutes. The scones should be light golden in color and firm to the touch.

How to serve

1 After baking, set the scones aside to cool and harden a little.

2 Cut in half. Spread with butter, then add some jam, and top it off with some fresh whipped or clotted cream. Delicious!

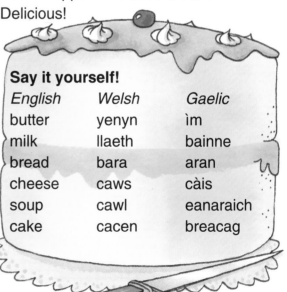

Say it yourself!

English	Welsh	Gaelic
butter	yenyn	ìm
milk	llaeth	bainne
bread	bara	aran
cheese	caws	càis
soup	cawl	eanaraich
cake	cacen	breacag

Life in Britain

WHERE PEOPLE LIVE

More than 80 percent of British people lives in towns and cities. Almost one in four live within 15.5 miles (25 km) of the center of London. The next biggest cities are Glasgow and Birmingham, each with a population of about 2,500,000. Although some people live in high-rise apartment buildings, many live in terraced or semidetached houses with a garden. One-story bungalows are also popular with retired people, many of whom often live along the south coast or in the southwest of England where the weather is usually milder.

Many people would like to live in villages, but it often costs too much to travel to work, school, and stores. Some of the smaller, pretty villages make money from selling teas, sovenirs, and antiques to summer visitors. Traditionally, there are two main types of village – the "long street," where all the buildings are placed beside the main road, and the "nucleated," where the houses are all clustered around a central point, such as the village green, pond, church, or inn.

WHAT PEOPLE DO

British agriculture is highly mechanized and efficient, so it doesn't need many workers. Major industries include making machinery, cars, aircraft, chemicals, and electronic goods. Most people work in offices, stores, schools, or hospitals. The fastest growing businesses are banking and tourism.

POLICE

There is no national police force in Britain. Instead, each county or major city has its own. There is also a separate force for the railroads. The biggest police force is London's Metropolitan Police. The emergency telephone number for the police, and the other emergency services, is 999.

GOING TO SCHOOL

British children have to go to school from the age of five until they are sixteen. Over 90 percent go to state schools where the education is paid for out of taxes. Some children go to independent schools for which their parents have to pay. These include some of the country's oldest and most famous boarding schools, such as Eton College which is over 500 years old. Some schools make pupils wear a uniform, and you can also find schools that will only take boys or girls. Those schools that take both, regardless of their abilities, are known as comprehensive schools. There are over 100 universities in Britain. The two oldest are Oxford and Cambridge.

KEEPING INFORMED

Because Britain is quite a small country, you can buy the same newspapers in every part of the country, although local editions will carry different sports news and advertisements. There are also many local newspapers.

The British Broadcasting Corporation (BBC) controls two television channels and five national radio networks. BBC Radio also runs a World Service which broadcasts in over 30 languages. Independent Television (ITV) also has two TV channels, and there is a satellite channel, Sky Television. There are also dozens of local radio stations.

SHOPPING

In Britain you can find Europe's largest shopping mall – the Metro Centre at Gateshead in the northeast of England. London has such famous department stores as Harrods and Selfridges as well as specialty shops like Hamleys (toys) and Virgin Megastore (CDs, videos, and games). The most famous High Street chain-stores are Marks & Spencer, W. H. Smith, and Boots. But old-fashioned open-air markets are still very popular in both towns and villages.

Say it yourself!

English	Welsh	Gaelic
police	heddlu	riaghladh baile
school	ysgol	sgoil
shop	siop	bùth
market	marchnad	margadh
work	gwaith	obair

Dressing the Part

The formal male attire of a suit with matching jacket, vest, and trousers is an English invention, as are the blazer and the bowler hat. London's Savile Row is the home of the world's best tailoring. Nearby Jermyn Street is where a gentleman gets his shirts and shoes made to measure, while younger people like to shop in the stores on King's Road in Chelsea, for the latest fashions.

Designers such as Mary Quant, Zandra Rhodes, Vivienne Westwood, and Bruce Oldfield have revolutionized Britain's standing in the world of high fashion.

The Princess of Wales has captured the headlines as one of the world's most stylishly dressed women.

THE CITY GENT

The true "city gent" is not such a common sight today, but he still represents many people's idea of the "typical Englishman."

SCOTTISH SPLENDOR

North of the border, you may come across men wearing kilts, usually for some ceremonial purpose. The tartan pattern worn depends on which clan (family) you belong to or which army regiment you have served in.

WELSH WOOLENS

The traditional dress worn by Welsh women to an *eisteddfod* (see page 25) is based on the fashions of the seventeenth century when housewives working at home would wear their woolen nightgown and an apron on top of a petticoat. When they went out, they would add a shawl and hat and, in winter, a hooded cloak.

BE A PEARLY!

YOU WILL NEED:

waistcoat

chalk

paper and pen

white buttons

An old garment to decorate* (denim shirt, jeans)

flat cap

needle, thread and thimble

1 Draw your design first on paper, and then copy it onto your garment with the chalk.

2 Following your pattern, sew the buttons on firmly.

3 Put on the vest or jacket and the flat cap, and you have your own "pearly" outfit.

PEARLY KINGS AND QUEENS

At the beginning of this century, most Londoners bought their fruit and vegetables from street markets. The stallholders were known as "costermongers" or "barrow boys." Costers had their own special language and dressed up to look really "pie and mash" (Flashy and smart).

Costers liked to decorate their vests with bright buttons made of brass or, better still, pearl. And the more buttons, the better. Soon every district of London's East End had its own "Pearly King and Queen." The "title" was passed down in families, and pearly kings and queens still exist today, although they only dress up in their full regalia to raise money for charity.

Say it yourself!

English	Welsh	Gaelic
shirt	crys	léine
shoe	esgid	bròg
hat	het	biorraid
trousers	trowsus	triubhas
jacket	siaced	seacaid

Made in Britain

Britain was the first country in the world to have an industrial revolution. The first iron bridge in the world (built in 1779) can be found at Ironbridge in central England. George Stephenson's famous locomotive, *Rocket*, built in 1829 is shown on the £5 banknote, and there is a picture of Michael Faraday, the pioneer of electricity, on the £20 note.

Here are some other important moments in British science and technology:

1687 Newton formulates laws of gravity and planetary motion.

1712 The first successful steam engine, the Dudley Castle Newcomen, is built.

1825 The first public railroad is opened between Stockton and Darlington in the north of England.

1863 The world's first underground railroad opens in London.

1876 The telephone is invented by Alexander Graham Bell.

1928 Alexander Fleming accidentally discovers penicillin, the first antibiotic.

1955 The hovercraft is patented.

1978 The world's first test-tube baby is born.

COMET AND CONCORDE

In 1919 two British pilots, Alcock and Brown, became the first men to fly the Atlantic in a British-built Vickers Vimy bomber. In 1930 inventor Frank Whittle patented a design for the first jet engine. In 1952 Britain became the first country to introduce regular jet passenger services in the De Havilland Comet. The Anglo-French Concorde, the world's first supersonic airliner, has been flying the Atlantic in three hours since 1976.

NORTH SEA OIL AND GAS

Gas was discovered under the North Sea in 1965 and oil in 1969. By 1977 almost all the gas used in Britain was coming from the North Sea, and by 1987 Britain had become the sixth largest oil producer in the world. The drilling rigs used to explore for oil and gas and then pump them ashore have to be able to stand up to winds of 161 mi/hr (260 km/h) and waves 98 ft (30 m high).

THE BEST CAR IN THE WORLD

Britain is the home of many historic high-performance cars such as the Aston-Martin, Austin-Healy, Lotus, M.G., Bentley, and Jaguar. But one name outshines them all.

In 1904 Mr. F. H. Royce, an engineer, met the Honorable C. S. Rolls, a car salesman. At the 1906 Motor Show they launched the Rolls Royce *Silver Ghost*. It had polished aluminum bodywork and real silver fittings. They put it on an endurance test to show that it was more than just beautiful to look at. It ran for 14,371 miles without a fault – doubling the previous record. The Rolls Royce record stood for more than fifty years, proving that the *Silver Ghost* was indeed the best car in the world.

Sport

Many sports originated in Great Britain. Cricket, soccer, rugby, tennis, squash, table tennis, badminton, canoeing, and snooker were all invented in Britain. The first rules for such sports as boxing, golf, hockey, yachting and horse racing also originated in Britain. The most popular sports that people take part in, rather than watching, are angling, snooker, and darts.

SOCCER

Soccer began as a contest between neighboring villages – with no limit to the number on each side, no fixed pitch, and almost no rules! The Soccer Association drew up the rules of the modern game in 1863, and in 1888 twelve clubs joined together to form the first Soccer League. England won the World Cup in 1966. English teams such as Tottenham Hotspur, Arsenal, Liverpool, and Manchester United have fans all around the world.

CRICKET

Cricket is very much the English game. At village level, a match can be played in an afternoon. At international level it can take five days – and still end in a draw. A form of cricket was being played 450 years ago. The first Australian team to visit England came in 1882 – and won!

HIGHLAND GAMES

Over 70 Highland Games meetings are held in Scotland each year. The most famous take place at Braemar in Aberdeenshire, Scotland, in September and are attended by the Royal family. Events include throwing the hammer and tossing the caber, a pole 20 feet (6 m) long, weighing over 110 pounds (50 kg).

RUGBY

Rugby and soccer became two separate sports when the rules laid down by the Soccer Association said that only the goalkeeper could handle the ball. Two kinds of rugby are played in Britain. Rugby Union is played by amateurs in teams of fifteen in the south of England and in Wales (where it is the national sport). Rugby League is played by professionals in teams of thirteen in the north of England.

GOLF

Golf may have been invented in Holland, but has been played in Scotland for at least 400 years. At first it was played with balls made of wood, then of leather stuffed with feathers. The earliest rules were drawn up in 1754 at the Royal and Ancient course in St Andrews.

TENNIS

Tennis was originally called "sphairistike"! The first rules were drawn up by the All England Croquet Club when it held its first tournament in the London suburb of Wimbledon in 1877. Wimbledon is still the world's most famous tennis event.

Play the Game!

DOMINOES

This is a traditional game played in pubs. Dominoes are normally made of wood or plastic, but you can make your own out of thick cardboard, marking the dots, as shown below, with a felt-tip pen. You will also need to bend some long pieces of cardboard to make racks so that you can see your own dominoes without letting your opponent see them.

There are many different ways of playing the game. This is one of the simplest.

1 Place the 28 domino cards face down on a table and mix them up.

2 Each player picks up one card. The one with the highest number of points gets to pick up the rest of his/her cards first and to start the game. Replace the two "draw" domino cards and mix them all up again.

3 Each player, in turn, picks up 14 cards apiece.

4 The first player lays down a card. Suppose it has 5 dots and 1 dot on it. The next player can put down either a domino with 5 dots , or one with 1 dot. If you can't go, you knock on the table and lose a turn.

5 Dominoes with two matching figures on them (3 + 3) are laid sideways across the line. To continue from this, you need another card with a 3 on it.

6 The game usually ends when one player has managed to use up all of his/her dominoes. If you end up with everyone not being able to go, add up the number of dots on the dominoes still held. The winner is the one with the lowest score.

TIDDLYWINKS

There are two basic versions. You will need 1 large button or counter and 6 small ones. It is best to play on a hard, smooth surface like a piece of board.

Version 1
1 Draw two parallel lines about 3 ft (1 m) apart to make a start and finish line.

2 Each player has 3 small buttons and, in turn, uses the large button to press firmly on the edge of the small buttons. This should make them jump forward.

3 The aim is to be the first to get 3 buttons behind the finish line.

Version 2

Instead of drawing two parallel lines, draw three or four circles one inside the other. Each ring can be given a different score. You can put an eggcup in the "bull's-eye" and give the highest score for getting the button into the cup.

You can make up your own versions of tiddlywinks. Some people play it blindfolded!

BRITISH BOBBY

This is a children's version of the game "shove ha'penny". You will need a large piece of thick paper 47 x 32 inches (120 x 80 cm) and a crayon. Mark the card into eight equal parts. Label the last one "London."

You can play this with buttons on a tabletop, or with a marble or table tennis ball on the floor.

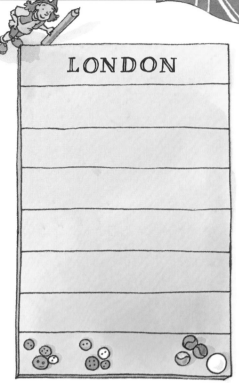

1 Players, in turn, slide the button/roll the marble/blow the ball from the edge of the paper farthest from "London."

2 If the button/marble/ball stops safely between two lines, you can draw the outline of a policeman's helmet and write your name inside it.

If it stops on a line or goes over the edge, there is no score. If it stops in "London," the player takes another turn.

3 The winner is the first one to get a helmet in five of the spaces, with no gaps between them.

Holidays and Festivals

More than a third of the population takes a foreign vacation each year. The main attraction is the guaranteed sunshine of the Mediterranean, and the most popular destinations are Spain, Greece, and Cyprus.

THEME PARKS

Specially built leisure attractions are quite new in Britain, but there are now more than 100 to be found. Alton Towers and Thorpe Park are like a giant funfair, while the Jorvik Center recreates what York was like in Viking times, even down to the smells. In Manchester you can tour the studios of Granada Television.

THE SEASIDE

The idea that sea bathing is good for you dates from about 1820. Brighton was the first seaside resort. Later, railroads made it possible for people to take cheap day trips to the coast. Piers were built so that people could walk out to sea and breathe in the salty air. There are seaside resorts all around the coast. The biggest one is Blackpool.

STATELY HOMES

The British love visiting old houses and castles, and there are thousands to choose from. Longleat, Chatsworth, and Blenheim Palace are some of the most famous. The most spectacular castles are in Wales (Caernarfon, Conway) and along the border between England and Scotland (Alnwick, Bamburgh).

MUSEUMS

In Britain a new museum opens every two weeks. London alone has more than 200, including museums about artillery, scouts, nursing, films and television, design, ships and the sea, the theater, transportation , toys, and musical instruments.

MAY DAY

The first day of May used to be a holiday to celebrate the coming of spring. People would go "maying" in the woods and collect green branches and blossoms to decorate their houses. A maypole was put up to dance around, and a young girl was chosen as "May Queen" to head a procession through the village or town. These celebrations are still held in different parts of England.

GUY FAWKES

On November 5, people light bonfires and set off fireworks in memory of Guy Fawkes who tried to blow up Parliament with barrels of gunpowder in 1605. Sometimes a "guy" made up of old clothes is burned on the fire.

BURNS NIGHT

On January 25 each year, some Scots hold banquets in honor of Robert Burns, Scotland's national poet. He wrote the words of "Auld Lang Syne," a song traditionally sung at New Year's.

The main course of the banquet is usually a haggis which is chopped meat, spices, and vegetables, all cooked in a sheep's stomach. It is carried to the table with great honor, accompanied by a Highland piper. It is served with "tatties" (potatoes) and "bashed neeps" (mashed turnips). The poet's health is toasted in whisky.

HOGMANAY

In Scotland the New Year celebrations (Hogmanay) are even more important than Christmas. At midnight people go "first footing" and visit the homes of friends with gifts which traditionally include a lump of coal and a silver coin.

EISTEDDFOD

Eisteddfod is the Welsh name for a festival of music, poetry, drama, and handicrafts. They have been held for over 1,000 years. The most important is the Royal National Eisteddfod which is held every August. The Welsh language is spoken in all the events.

NOTTING HILL CARNIVAL

The idea of a street carnival came to Britain from Trinidad. For thirty years, a carnival has been organized by Afro-Caribbean people living in the Notting Hill district of west London. It is held on the last weekend in August and attracts up to 500,000 people – making it Europe's largest street event.

The Arts

GREAT WRITERS

Britain is probably best known for its literature. Many of the characters created by British writers are well known even in countries that do not speak English as their main language. These include Robin Hood, Sherlock Holmes, James Bond, Winnie the Pooh, and Peter Rabbit. English poetry is also well known, through the works of such poets as Keats, Shelley, Byron and Browning.

William Shakespeare (1564–1616)
Shakespeare is probably the world's most famous playwright. He wrote 36 plays, including *Hamlet* and *Romeo and Juliet*. Shakespeare also acted in plays and was one of the owners of a theater called the Globe. This has been rebuilt in London so that people can see how plays were acted in his day – in daylight, and open to the sky!

British Winners of the Nobel Prize for Literature	
1907	Rudyard Kipling
1932	John Galsworthy
1948	T. S. Eliot
1950	Bertrand Russell
1953	Sir Winston Churchill
1983	William Golding

Charles Dickens (1812–70)
In his novels, Dickens invented such characters as Oliver Twist and Mr. Pickwick. When he was young, Dickens wanted to be an actor. After he became famous, he used to give public readings from his books. He is buried in "Poets' Corner" in Westminster Abbey. A portrait of Dickens appears on the £10 banknote.

Dylan Thomas (1914–53)
Dylan Thomas was a Welsh poet who wrote in English. His most famous poem is *Under Milk Wood* which describes the people of a Welsh seaside village.

Shakespeare's Globe Theatre stood on the south bank of the Thames.

Sir Christopher Wren rebuilt St. Paul's between 1675 and 1710.

DESIGN

Sir Christopher Wren (1632–1723)
Sir Christopher Wren helped to rebuild London after the Great Fire of 1666. His most famous building is St Paul's Cathedral, but he also designed over fifty churches.

MUSIC TODAY

In Wales there are competitions for male voice choirs and some in the north of England for brass bands. In Scotland the bands feature drums, flutes, and bagpipes.

The composer Sir Edward Elgar (1857–1934) is well known for ceremonial music such as *Pomp and Circumstance,* and for choral/orchestral works. Many music societies also perform the comic operas composed by Sir William Gilbert (1836–1911) and Sir Arthur Sullivan (1842–1900), one of the most popular being *The Mikado.*

Britain's most famous modern composer is Benjamin Britten (1913–76). He started a famous annual music festival at Aldeburgh in Suffolk.

Josiah Wedgwood (1730-95)

Wedgwood pottery is famous around the world. Many of the designs are based on carvings from ancient Greece and Pompeii.

ART

English painting was at its best between 1750 and 1850. John Constable (1776–1837) and Joseph Turner (1775–1851) were both excellent landscape painters.

John Constable painted scenes of the Suffolk countryside. He sketched outdoors in summer and painted in his studio in winter.

Say it yourself!

English	Welsh	Gaelic
book	llyfr	leabhar
picture	darlun	dealbh
music	miwsig	ceòl

British History

Britain is steeped with history. Here are just a few of the key events.

THE ENGLISH

The ancestors of the modern English are the Angles, Saxons, and Jutes. They came from the area where Germany, Holland, and Denmark now meet. They began to settle in England from the fifth century A.D. and drove the native British into Wales. During Anglo-Saxon times, England was raided by Vikings from Denmark and Norway. In the end many of them came to settle, too. Most villages in England got their names from the Anglo-Saxons or the Vikings.

THE ROMANS

The Roman conquest of Britain began in A.D.43. Roman rule lasted for almost 400 years. They founded London, York, Lincoln, and Chester, but they never conquered Scotland. On the orders of the Emperor Hadrian, they built a wall right across the country to stop Scottish raids.

THE NORMANS

In 1066 England was invaded by Normans (Vikings who had settled in France). The last Anglo-Saxon king, Harold, was completely defeated at the Battle of Hastings. The Normans built many castles, and French became the language of the rulers until about 1400. Many French words were added to the English language.

ELIZABETH I (1533–1603)

Many people think that Elizabeth I was England's greatest ruler. She was very hardworking and spoke French, Italian, Greek, Latin, and Welsh. In 1588 her navy defeated the great Armada sent by Spain to conquer England.

EMPIRE

In 1607 English people founded Jamestown in Virginia and began to settle in America. Although the American colonies became independent after 1776, Britain's empire continued to grow until it became the biggest in the history of the world. The colony with the biggest population was India. The biggest in area were Canada and Australia.

	Time Band
A.D. 43	Roman conquest begins.
871-99	Alfred the Great reconquers England from the Vikings.
1066	The Norman conquest.
1215	King John signs the Magna Carta
1485	Tudor victory at the Battle of Bosworth ends the "Wars of the Roses."
1536	Henry VIII makes himself the head of the Church of England.
1603	James VI of Scotland becomes king of England as well.
1666	Great Fire of London destroys a major part of the city.
1707	Act of Union joins England, Scotland, and Wales under one parliament.
1805	Admiral Nelson wins the Battle of Trafalgar.
1837-1901	Reign of Queen Victoria; Britain becomes leading world power.
1947	Independence of India means the beginning of the end of the British Empire.
1973	Britain joins the European Economic Community.

INDUSTRIAL REVOLUTION

Britain was the first country to develop industries based on steam power and organized factories. In 1851 a "Great Exhibition" was held in Hyde Park in London to show off Britain's industrial power. This was the world's first international fair.

SIR WINSTON CHURCHILL (1874-1965)

Churchill was the most famous Englishman of the twentieth century. As a young man, he was an army officer who fought in India and Africa. Then he went into politics and was a great public speaker. He was prime minister from 1940 to 1945 (during World War II), and again from 1951 to 1955. He also wrote many history books and won the Nobel Prize for literature.

Say it yourself!

English	Welsh	Gaelic
history	hanes	eachdraidh
king	brenin	rìgh
battle	brwdyr	cath
castle	castell	daingneach

29

Round Britain Race

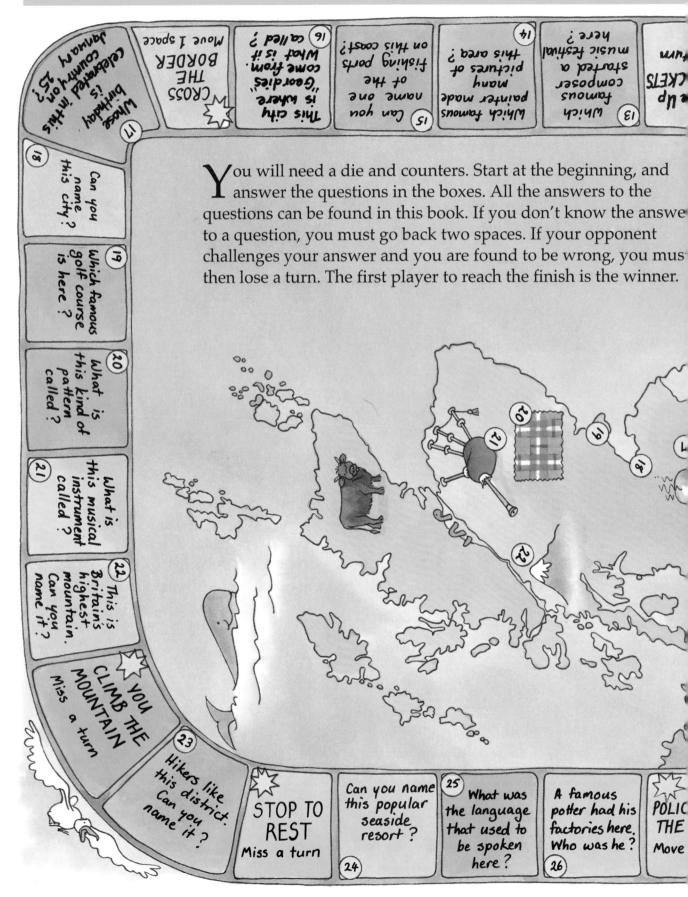

You will need a die and counters. Start at the beginning, and answer the questions in the boxes. All the answers to the questions can be found in this book. If you don't know the answer to a question, you must go back two spaces. If your opponent challenges your answer and you are found to be wrong, you must then lose a turn. The first player to reach the finish is the winner.

13 Which famous composer started a music festival here?

14 Which famous painter made many pictures of this area?

15 Can you name one of the fishing ports on this coast?

16 This city is where "Geordies" come from. What is it called?

CROSS THE BORDER
Move 1 space

17 Whose birthday is celebrated in this country on January 25?

18 Can you name this city?

19 Which famous golf course is here?

20 What is this kind of pattern called?

21 What is this musical instrument called?

22 This is Britain's highest mountain. Can you name it?

YOU CLIMB THE MOUNTAIN
Miss a turn

23 Hikers like this district. Can you name it?

STOP TO REST
Miss a turn

24 Can you name this popular seaside resort?

25 What was the language that used to be spoken here?

26 A famous potter had his factories here. Who was he?

POLIC... THE ... Move

Board game map — "UK / Europe" quiz game

START 🖐

HOME 🐕

TAKE THE FERRY — Move 1 space

1. What is this kind of snack called?
2. What drink is made here?
3. Can you name the kind of cheese made here?
4. This area is popular with tourists. Can you name it?
5. Can you name this island?
6. Can you name this river?
7. You can cross to France here on a British invention.
8. What kinds of foods is this country famous for?
9. This is the county the English call it. It's "garden". What name?
10. Can you name the festival held here in August?
11. What is the name of the giant skyscraper built here?
12. Can you name te tour held...

28. What does the flag of this country look like?
29. What is this mountainous region called?
30. Can you name this city?
31. Shakespeare was born here. What is this town called?

...is ...tional ...e of ...ntry?

Index

Additional Photographs:
Bridgeman P. 26, 27, 28;
Camera Press P. 16, 29; J.
Allan Cash Ltd. P. 10, 15,
Cover; Eye Ubiquitous P. 6, 9,
14, 15, 28, Cover; Chris
Fairclough P. 7, 9, 14, 20;
Robert Harding P. 17, 18, 24,
25; P. MacDonald P. 7; Frank
Spooner P.8; Zefa P. 7, 19.

Index